Twenty to Make

Sugar Animals

Frances McNaughton

ch Press

First published in Great Britain 2009

Search Press Limited
Wellwood, North Farm Road,
Tunbridge Wells, Kent TN2 3DR

Reprinted 2009

Text copyright © Frances McNaughton 2009

Photographs by Debbie Patterson at
Search Press Studios

Photographs and design copyright
© Search Press Ltd 2009

ISBN: 978-1-84448-478-2

Suppliers
If you have difficulty in obtaining any of the
materials and equipment mentioned in this book,
then please visit the Search Press website for
details of suppliers: www.searchpress.com

Printed in Malaysia

*This book is dedicated to
my lovely Mum, and to Jack,
Ruby and Harvey.*

Contents

Introduction

The animals in this book are made using techniques suitable for beginners, with a few more detailed models for the more advanced. The basic shapes and tools are kept as simple as possible.

I made my animals in sugarpaste, coloured with strong paste food colours. Sugarpaste is available from many supermarkets and sugarcraft shops. It can be made stronger by kneading in a small pinch of CMC (cellulose gum) or gum tragacanth. This will help to make the model sit up without flopping.

The amount of paste I have listed for each model is only intended as a guide – models can, of course, be made in different sizes.

White marzipan can also be used to make the models, coloured in the same way as sugarpaste. Chocolate sugarpastes and edible modelling pastes are a good way of making brown and cream models and parts without having to use food colours.

Ready-coloured sugarpaste and edible modelling paste, and the other items mentioned above are available from specialist sugarcraft shops and online sugarcraft and cake decorating suppliers.

The techniques in this book can also be used to make long-lasting model animals with non-edible modelling pastes such as air drying modelling pastes available from craft shops.

Basic shapes

1 Ball

It is a good idea to start each shape by making a smooth ball shape first. Knead the paste until smooth and roll it between the palms of your hands to shape a ball with no visible cracks.

2 Oval or egg shape

Roll the ball in the palms of your hands to make it longer.

3 Cone

Roll the ball at one end in the palms of your hands.

4 Pear (used for some of the heads)

Roll the ball at one end between your fingers.

5 Sausage

Roll the ball with your hands to make the sausage.

6 Round-ended sausage (used for some of the legs)

Roll one side of the ball to make a sausage, leaving one end fatter.

7 Long, pointed oval (used for some of the bodies)

Roll the ball to form two narrow ends.

8 Carrot

Roll the ball to form a long, pointed cone.

9 Candy stick (used as a support)

These can be bought from sweet shops. When the packet is first opened, the candy sticks can be a bit too soft, so lay them out to dry for a few days, until hard. They can also be made in advance from strengthened sugarpaste: knead a pinch of CMC into 50g (1¾oz) of sugarpaste. Roll to form thin sausages and cut to 6cm (2³/₈in). Leave to dry in a warm, dry place for a few days, until hard.

Joining shapes

Join the pieces of each model together as they are made, while still soft, by dampening the surfaces with a small paintbrush dipped in water. Try not to over-wet the paste or the pieces will slide off rather than stick.

Basic tools

Heart cutter, 2.5cm (1in)
For cutting out faces.

Tiny blossom cutter
For cutting out the Leopard's
and the Giraffe's spots (see
pages 32–33 and 44–45).

Cocktail stick/toothpick
For making marks and shaping
small pieces of sugarpaste.

Sharp pointed scissors
For cutting sugarpaste.

Drinking straw, cut off at an angle
This is used to make curved marks for
mouths and other details.

Thin palette knife
This is available from sugarcraft and
art shops. It is useful for releasing
sugarpaste from the work surface, and
for cutting and marking lines.

Other equipment

Non-stick workboard

Small rolling pin

Small paintbrush or **water brush** Used for dampening the sugarpaste to
join pieces together.

Vegetable cooking oil To stop paste sticking to your hands and tools, rub
a small amount of oil in to your hands and work surface.

Icing sugar Alternatively, sprinkle a small amount of icing sugar on your
hands and work surface. Be careful not to use too much, as this could dry the
paste and cause cracking.

Plastic sandwich bags For storing pieces of paste to keep them soft, and for
rolling paste flat, as for the Leopard's spots (see page 33).

Elephant

Materials:

90g (3oz) pale lilac sugarpaste
Candy stick

Tools:

Cocktail stick
Drinking straw
Sharp pointed scissors
Thin palette knife

Instructions:

1 Divide the paste in half and use half for the body: make an egg shape with a candy stick for support.

2 Snip a tiny pointed tail with scissors.

3 Divide the second half of the paste into four: one for the head, one for the arms and two for the legs.

4 For the legs, make two short cones. Pinch gently around the fat end to make the flat foot. Mark three toes on the edge of each foot using the end of a drinking straw. Attach the legs to the body.

5 For the arms, make one sausage. Pinch gently round each end to flatten. Mark three toes on each end with a drinking straw. Stick the arms on to the top of the body.

6 Make a ball for the head, half the size of the body. Roll the end between your fingers to form the trunk. Use the cocktail stick to mark two holes at the end for the nostrils. Mark a few lines across the trunk to make it look wrinkled.

7 Curve the trunk up. Snip a pointed mouth under the trunk with scissors. Use a cocktail stick to mark the eyes.

8 Squeeze each side of the fat part of the head between finger and thumb to make two large ears.

9 Attach the head to the body.

The little elephant is the same as the main one, made smaller and with purple sugarpaste.

Panda

Materials:

35g (1¼oz) white sugarpaste
30g (1oz) black sugarpaste
Tiny piece of pink sugarpaste
Candy stick

Tools:

Cocktail stick
Drinking straw
Sharp pointed scissors
Thin palette knife
Heart cutter, 2.5cm (1in)

Instructions:

1 Divide the white paste into about 25g (just under 1oz) for the body, 10g (⅓oz) for the head and a pea-sized piece for the cheeks and eyes.

2 Make the body into an egg shape with a candy stick for support (not shown).

3 Divide the black paste into four balls: two for the legs, one for the arms and one for the face, nose, ears, eyes and tail.

4 For the legs, form two of the black balls into pear shapes. Shape a foot at the fat end. Mark claws with a cocktail stick. Attach the narrow end of each leg to the body.

5 For the arms, make one long sausage from the other black ball. Stick on top of the body.

6 Make the head from a ball of white paste, approximately half the size of the body.

7 Cut out a black heart shape for the face, using the heart cutter.

8 Attach an oval of white on to the heart shape. Mark two curves, side by side, for the mouth, using a drinking straw.

9 Make a black triangle for the nose.

10

10 For the eyes, press two tiny balls of white and then two even smaller balls of black on to the heart shape. Stick the face on to the head. Attach the head on to the top of the body.

11 For the ears, make two small balls of black paste and shape them to make indents.

12 Make the tail from a small ball of black paste.

13 Stick on three small pink balls to each foot for the toe pads, and a larger one for the sole of the foot.

The baby panda is just a smaller version of its mum, lying in a more relaxed position. It has a pink nose to make it extra cute.

Lizard

Materials:

15g (½oz) black sugarpaste
10g (⅓oz) blue sugarpaste
Pea-sized piece of yellow sugarpaste
Tiny pieces of red and black sugarpaste

Tools:

Cocktail stick
Sharp pointed scissors
Thin palette knife

Instructions:

1 Set aside a tiny piece of the black paste for the eyes.

2 Make the legs from four large pea-sized pieces of blue paste rolled into sausage shapes. Bend each to form a knee and foot. Cut each foot with scissors to form three toes.

3 For the body, join the main ball of black paste to the remaining ball of blue paste and roll to form a long carrot shape. The blue end should form a point. Roll the black end between your fingers to form a neck and head. Flatten the nose end slightly. Mark nostrils with a cocktail stick.

4 Attach the legs on to the underside of the body, feet pointing forward.

5 Roll two thin yellow sausages, slightly shorter than the body. Stick on top of the body to look like stripes.

6 For the eyes, make two small balls of red paste, and two smaller balls of black and stick together on to the sides of the head.

Snakes

Materials:

Large pea-sized pieces of red, yellow and
black sugarpaste

Tools:

Thin palette knife
Cocktail stick

Instructions:

1 For the head, make a small cone shape and flatten the narrow end. Mark the
nostrils with a cocktail stick. Attach two tiny black eyes (not shown).

2 Roll two or three different colours of paste into thin sausages.

3 Cut each sausage into small segments. Join the different-coloured segments
back together to form stripes.

4 Roll gently with your hand to form a smooth sausage for the body with a thin
point for the tail. Shape the body by bending or coiling it up.

5 Attach the head.

Hippopotamus

Materials:

50g (1¾oz) purple
   sugarpaste
Tiny pieces of white and
   black sugarpaste
Candy stick

Tools:

Thin palette knife
Sharp pointed scissors
Cocktail stick

Instructions:

1 Divide the paste; about 15g (½oz)
for the head and ears, and 35g (1¼oz)
for the body. To make the body, shape
a ball of purple paste in the palm of
your hand to form a long oval.

2 Cut into the narrow ends to make the legs.

3 Bend the whole body to form a curve, and to
stand upright on the legs. Push a candy stick in
at the top of the front legs to support the head
(not shown).

4 Snip a small tail with scissors.

5 For the head, break off a tiny piece of paste
and save it to make the ears. Make a fat pear shape for the
head. Mark two nostrils, and mark the mouth using a knife.

6 For the eyes, make two tiny, flattened balls of white, and
press on two smaller balls of black. Stick on to the face.

7 Attach the head on to the body.

8 Make two tiny balls for the ears from the remaining purple
sugarpaste. Shape the indents and attach the ears to the head.

Make a baby hippopotamus by reducing all the sizes and using pink sugarpaste.

Dolphin

Materials:

15g (½oz) each of blue and pale blue sugarpaste

Tiny piece of black sugarpaste

Tools:

Sharp pointed scissors or thin palette knife

Cocktail stick

Instructions:

1 For the fins, shape three small pea-sized pieces of blue paste into small carrot shapes. Flatten and curve them slightly.

2 Make a smooth ball from the blue paste and one from the pale blue paste. Roll each between your hands to form pointed sausage shapes. Join them gently together by rolling.

3 Roll one end of the dolphin between your fingers to form the narrow nose. To make the tail, roll the other end of the dolphin between your fingers and flatten it slightly.

4 Cut into the centre of the flattened end about 1cm ($^3/_8$in) with the scissors or knife. Flatten and shape the points of the tail.

5 Attach one of the fins on the back and one on each side. Curve the tips towards the tail. Mark a blowhole with a cocktail stick.

6 Make the eyes from two tiny balls of black paste and attach them.

Make a baby dolphin to swim alongside its mother, using purple sugarpaste.

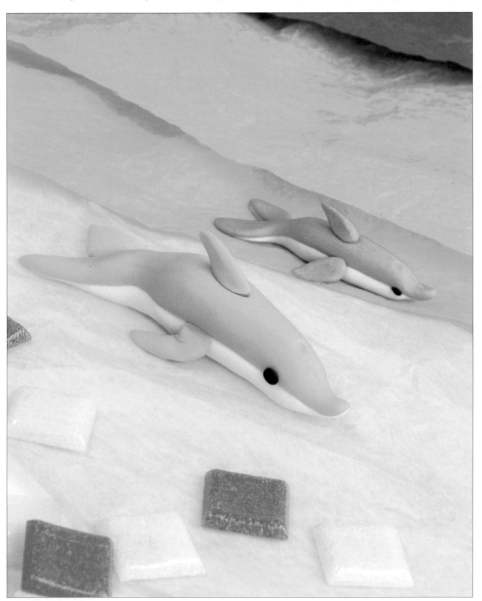

Kangaroo

Materials:

50g (1¾oz) orange sugarpaste
Pea-sized piece of white sugarpaste
Tiny piece of black sugarpaste
Candy stick

Tools

Thin palette knife
Cocktail stick
Drinking straw

Instructions:

1 Divide the orange paste in two and use about half for the body. Shape a ball of paste in the palm of your hand to form a long, fat carrot shape. Roll one end to make a long, pointed tail. Bend the body to make it stand up. Push in a candy stick to support the head (not shown). Divide the rest of the orange paste into: a large pea-sized ball for the arms and another piece. Divide the other piece into three for the legs, arms and head.

2 For the tummy, make a flattened oval of white paste and attach it to the body.

3 To make the legs, roll two balls of the orange paste between your fingers to leave a fat end. Flatten the fat end and mark toes at the thin end with a knife. Roll the fat end towards the thin end and attach the legs to the body.

4 For the arms, roll one small sausage. Mark the paws at each end using a cocktail stick. Stick the arms on top of the body.

5 To make the ears, break off a tiny piece of paste and make two small carrot shapes. Flatten them in the middle with a cocktail stick.

6 Use a ball of orange paste to make a pear shape for the head. At the narrow end, mark the mouth with a drinking straw.

7 Make the nose from a small triangle of black paste.

8 Make the eyes from two tiny black balls of paste. Attach the eyes and nose to the head.

9 Attach the head to the body. Stick the ears on to the back of the head.

The joey is made from yellow sugarpaste in a smaller size, and he is in a slightly different position to make him look inquisitive!

Camel

Materials:

45g (1½oz) brown or chocolate
   sugarpaste
Tiny pieces of white and black sugarpaste
Candy stick

Tools:

Thin palette knife
Sharp pointed scissors
Cocktail stick

Instructions:

1 Divide the brown paste, taking about 20g (²/₃oz) for the body. Make it into a ball and then an oval shape. Press gently in the middle.

2 Pinch the paste up to form two humps. Make a few snips into the top of the humps with scissors. Divide the rest of the paste into about 10g (¹/₃oz) for the head, ears and tail, and divide what is left into five: four for the legs and one for the neck.

3 To make the legs, make four large pea shapes and roll to form sausages with fat ends. Cut a line down into the fat end to form a hoof. Attach the legs under the body.

4 For the neck, cut the candy stick to the height of the humps. Wrap the stick in brown paste, pressing the join together. Make little snips along the join with scissors. Attach the back of the neck to the body, with the snips facing the front.

5 Break off a small amount of the remaining brown paste and save it for the ears and tail. Make a pointed cone shape for the head. At the narrow end, mark the nostrils with a cocktail stick. Cut a mouth with scissors. Make the ears with two small balls, shape the indents and attach them to the head.

6 For the eyes, make two tiny flattened balls of white, and press on two smaller balls of black. A tiny carrot shape of black can be used for each eyelid.

7 Stick the eyes and eyelids on to the face. Attach the head on top of the neck.

8 For the mane, make a tiny sausage of paste. Flatten it down one side. Stick it over the top and back of the head. Snip into the edge with scissors to make it look like fur.

9 To make the tail, make a small sausage and flatten one end. Snip the flattened end to make it look like long fur. Join the tail to the body.

Tiger

Materials:

35g (1¼oz) orange sugarpaste

Small pieces of black, white and
  pink sugarpaste

Candy stick

Tools:

Fine palette knife

Cocktail stick

Heart cutter, 2.5cm (1in)

Sharp pointed scissors

Instructions:

1 Divide the orange paste, taking about 20g (²/₃oz) for the body. Make
a long, pointed oval. Cut into the ends to make the legs. Smooth the cut
edges. Mark the toes with a cocktail stick. Push in a short candy stick (not
shown) at the top of the front legs to support the head. Divide the rest of
the paste into a large pea size for the tail, and what is left for the head.

2 Make the tail from a long sausage with a black piece rolled into the end.

3 Make a ball for the head.

4 Make stripes from black sugarpaste by
rolling very thin, pointed sausages 2cm (¾in)
long. Stick them across the body, legs, tail
and head. Attach the tail to the body.

5 To make the face, cut out a black heart with the heart cutter and flatten the edge slightly to widen it. Cut out a white heart and press on top of the black one, so the edge of the black shows. Stick on to the head.

6 Attach two small white ovals for the cheeks, a small black triangle for the nose, and two tiny black eyes. Use a cocktail stick to mark whiskers in the cheeks.

7 Stick the head on to the body at the top of the front legs.

8 For the ears, make two small balls of black and two smaller balls of white. Press the white gently on to the black.

9 Make two small sausages of white and flatten along the edges. Join the fat edge down the sides of the head. Make snips along the edges using the scissors to make them look fluffy.

10 To make the back paws, make two small balls of pink. On each one, press three tiny pink balls for the toes. Stick into place.

Seal

Materials:

20g (²/₃oz) grey sugarpaste
Small amount of black sugarpaste

Tools:

Thin palette knife
Sharp pointed scissors
Drinking straw
Cocktail stick

Instructions:

1 To make the flippers, make two small cones and flatten slightly. Mark the wide end with a knife.

2 Roll the rest of the paste to form a long carrot shape.

3 Cut into the pointed end using the scissors to form the tail. Flatten it slightly. Roll the other end between your fingers to form a head. With the tail on the work surface, bend the body upwards.

4 Mark the lower part of the face with a drinking straw to form the cheeks, and add dots with a cocktail stick to look like whiskers. Mark the tail with a knife.

5 Attach the front flippers.

6 Stick on a small black triangle for the nose, and two small black eyes.

You can make a baby seal with white sugarpaste. This one is smaller than the adult and has a slightly simpler shape.

Skunk

Materials:

25g (just under 1oz) black sugarpaste
Small amount of white sugarpaste
Tiny piece of pink sugarpaste

Tools:

Fine palette knife
Drinking straw
Cocktail stick

Instructions:

1 Divide the black paste, taking about 15g (½oz) for the body. Make this into a long pointed oval. Cut into both the ends to make the legs.

2 Bend the back legs under the body. Smooth the cut edges.

3 Divide the rest of the paste into two – one part for the head and one for the tail. To make the tail, make a long thin pointed cone and flatten it with your fingers.

4 Attach the tail to the back of the body. Make a cone for the head. Mark the mouth with a drinking straw.

5 Attach the head at the top of the front legs. Attach a tiny pink ball for the nose.

6 Roll two thin white sausages, slightly shorter than the body and tail. Stick on top of the body, from the nose to the tail, to look like stripes. Press gently into position. Bend the tail up towards the head.

7 Make two small black balls and shape them into ears. Attach them to the head.

8 Mark the eyes with a cocktail stick.

You can make a squirrel using the same method. Use orange sugarpaste and make the squirrel stand more upright than the skunk. Add an oval of white sugarpaste for the tummy, leave out the stripes and add a brown nose.

Racoon

Materials:

20g (²/₃oz) grey sugarpaste
Small amounts of black and white sugarpaste

Tools

Fine palette knife
Drinking straw
Cocktail stick

Instructions:

1 Divide the grey paste in half. Use one half to make a long, pointed oval for the body. Cut into the ends to make the legs.

2 Bend the back legs under the body. Smooth the cut edges. Mark toes. Divide the rest of the grey into two pieces – one for the head, one for the tail.

3 For the tail, make two thin sausages, grey and black. Cut them into small segments, place them in alternate colours and join them back together. Roll gently to make a smooth, striped tail. Join on to the back end of the body.

4 To make the head, form a ball into a slightly triangular shape.

5 Make two small white cones and two smaller black cones and press them on to the face to look a like a mask.

6 To make the cheeks, stick on a small ball of white and mark with a drinking straw.

7 Attach a small black triangle for the nose.

8 To make the eyes, press on two tiny flattened balls of white and two smaller balls of black on top.

9 Join the head on to the body at the top of the front legs.

10 Make the ears from two small grey cones. Indent the middle with a cocktail stick. Attach to the head.

Leopard

Materials:

40g (1¹/₃oz) pale lemon or ivory sugarpaste
  (you could use white chocolate or marzipan)

Small amounts of white, brown and
  black sugarpaste

Candy stick

Tools:

Small rolling pin and plastic sandwich bag

Tiny blossom cutter

Cocktail stick

Thin palette knife

Sharp pointed scissors

Instructions:

1 Divide the pale lemon paste, taking about 25g (just under 1oz) for the body. Form this into a long, pointed oval. Cut into the ends, to make the legs.

2 Bend the back legs under the body. Smooth the cut edges. Mark toes. Push in a short candy stick (not shown) at the top of the front legs, to support the head. Divide the rest of the paste into about 10g (¹/₃oz) for the head and 5g (¹/₆oz) for the tail.

3 Form the tail piece into a long sausage and roll a tiny black piece into the end. Attach the tail to the body.

4 Form the head from a ball shape.

5 Form two small white ovals for the cheeks and attach these. For the ears, make two small balls of brown and two smaller balls of white. Press the white gently on to the brown. Dampen the head and stick the ears on.

6 Add a small black triangle for the nose and two tiny black eyes.

7 Join the head on to the body at the top of the front legs.

8 Roll out brown sugarpaste with a small rolling pin. If you roll the paste inside a plastic sandwich bag, it can be rolled quite thinly without sticking to the rolling pin or surface.

9 Cut out tiny brown blossoms with the cutter. Stick them all over the leopard.

This leopard is stretching out with a little cub, made in exactly the same way with smaller amounts of sugarpaste.

Koala

Materials:

65g (2¼oz) lilac sugarpaste

Small amounts of white and black
  sugarpaste

Candy stick

Tools:

Drinking straw

Sharp pointed scissors

Thin palette knife

Heart cutter, 2.5cm (1in)

Instructions:

1 Divide the lilac sugarpaste, taking about 25g (just under 1oz) for the body, then form this into an egg shape and add a candy stick for support (not shown). Stick on a white heart shape for the tummy. Divide the rest of the lilac paste into four balls.

2 Take two of the balls and form each one into a carrot shape to make the legs. Mark toes with a knife. Attach the legs.

3 Divide one of the balls into two and make smaller carrot shapes for the arms. Mark the paws with a knife. Join the arms to the body.

4 The last lilac ball makes the head. Mark the mouth with a drinking straw. Attach the head to the body.

5 Make two small white ovals for the ears. Stick on the sides of the head, pushing in gently to cup them. Snip around the edges with scissors.

6 Make the nose from a black oval shape and the eyes from two tiny balls of black paste.

The little koala is made in white with a lilac tummy, and seems to be waving a paw!

Lion

Materials:

50g (1¾oz) golden yellow sugarpaste

15g (½oz) orange sugarpaste

Small amounts of black and
  brown sugarpaste

Candy stick

Tools:

Cocktail stick

Sharp pointed scissors

Thin palette knife

Heart cutter, 2.5cm (1in)

Instructions:

1 Divide the yellow paste, taking about 25g (just under 1oz) for the body. Form this into an egg shape and add a candy stick for support. Divide the rest of the paste into about 5g (1/6oz) each for the front legs, tail and face, and the rest for the back legs.

2 Form the piece for the back legs into two cones. Flatten them slightly, mark toes with a cocktail stick and join them on to the body.

3 For the front legs, attach two sausage shapes, the same height as the body. Mark lines on the end of each foot to form paws.

4 To make the mane, form a ball of orange paste and squash it slightly to make a fat circle. Mark soft indents around the edge with a cocktail stick. Attach it to the top of the body.

5 For the face, cut out a heart shape from yellow paste, using the heart cutter. Save a small piece of paste for the ears. Stick the heart shape on to the mane.

6 Make the cheeks from two small yellow ovals. Mark them with a cocktail stick for the whiskers and attach them to the heart-shaped face.

7 Form the nose from a small triangle of brown paste and the eyes from two tiny balls of black paste. Attach these to the face.

8 Make the ears from two small balls of yellow paste. Stick them on to the head, cupping them at the same time.

9 Make a long, thin sausage for the tail. Flatten one end slightly, then cut with a knife or scissors to make the end look fluffy. Attach the tail.

The lioness is made in the same way, but the head is made from a yellow ball as she does not have a mane.

Crocodile

Materials:

50g (1¾oz) green sugarpaste

Small amounts of white and
   black sugarpaste

Tools:

Cocktail stick

Drinking straw

Sharp pointed scissors

Thin palette knife

Instructions:

1 Make four pea-sized pieces for the feet.
Roll each to make a small cone. Flatten
slightly. Mark the toes with a knife.

2 To make the eyes, take one small pea-
sized piece of green, press on a slightly
smaller ball of white, then press on an even smaller
ball of black. Cut the whole ball in half across the top.

3 Use the rest of the green paste to form a long pointed carrot shape
for the body. The pointed end will form the tail. Roll the fatter end of the
body between your fingers to form the head, and flatten it slightly.

4 Mark the mouth with a knife, and make two nostrils by pressing in the
point of a cocktail stick.

5 Use scissors to mark small 'v' shapes down the crocodile's back.

6 Join the legs to the sides of the body.

7 Stick the cut edges of the eyes on top of the head.

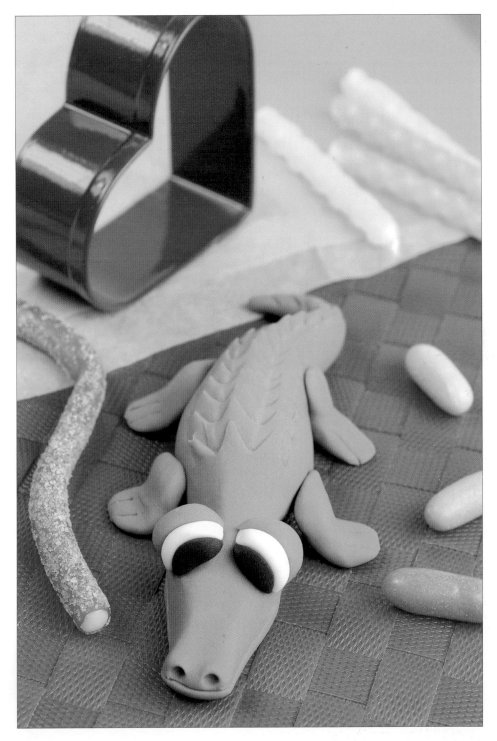

Monkey

Materials:

100g (3½oz) brown or chocolate sugarpaste

20g (⅔oz) peach sugarpaste

Small amount of black sugarpaste

Candy stick

Tools:

Cocktail stick

Sharp pointed scissors

Thin palette knife

Heart cutter, 2.5cm (1in)

Instructions:

1 Divide the brown paste, taking about 35g (1¼oz) to make an egg shape for the body. A hardened candy stick can be pushed right into the body, leaving a small piece at the top to help support the head.

2 Make a thin sausage of brown paste for the tail. Coil up the end and attach to the bottom of the body.

3 Take a pea-sized piece of brown paste for the ears, and press a smaller ball of peach on top. Cut in half across the top. Divide the rest of the brown paste into five equal balls.

4 Make four of the brown balls into long sausages for the legs and arms. Bend each in the middle for the knees and elbow.

5 Make four hands from small peach-coloured cones. Flatten slightly, and cut one long thumb and four fingers on each. Make two left- and two right-handed.

6 Attach the legs and arms to the body. Stick on the hands.

7 Take the fifth brown ball for the head and attach it to the body. Position the arms as shown.

8 Dampen the cut edge of the ears and attach to the side of the head.

9 For the face, cut out a heart shape in peach, using the heart cutter. Stick a small oval of peach at the bottom of the heart. Mark a wide mouth with a knife. Mark nostrils with a cocktail stick.

10 Stick on eyes made from two tiny balls of black and attach the face to the head.

Zebra

Materials:

For this model you will need to use strengthened edible modelling paste (see page 4)

35g (1¼oz) white edible modelling paste

35g (1¼oz) red edible modelling paste

Five candy sticks

10g (⅓oz) black sugarpaste

Tools:

Cocktail stick

Sharp pointed scissors

Thin palette knife

Instructions:

1 Take four candy sticks for the legs. Make four thin sausages of black paste and stick one around the middle of each leg.

2 Break the remaining candy stick for the neck so that it is shorter than the legs.

3 Shape the red modelling paste into a drum. Stick four pea-sized pieces of black paste on top. Use one of the candy sticks to push a hole down through each black ball, ready for inserting the legs.

4 Push each leg through a black ball and right down through the drum, to the work surface underneath. Make sure they all stand straight.

5 For the body, make 25g (just under 1oz) of white modelling paste into an oval shape.

6 For the head, make 10g (⅓oz) of white modelling paste into a small pear shape.

7 Make stripes from thin, pointed sausages of black. Stick these on to the body.

8 Stick a flattened black oval on to the thin end of the head, for the nose. Mark the nostrils with a cocktail stick.

9 Make eyes from two tiny black balls and stick these to the face.

10 Dampen the top and bottom of the candy-stick neck. Push one end into the body, so that it is sticking straight up. Gently push the head on to the top of the neck. Add a black stripe round the base of the neck.

11 Make ears from two small balls of black and stick them on top of the head. Shape them as shown.

12 For the mane, make a small sausage of black and flatten it down one side. Stick the fat edge over the top of the head, between the ears. Make small snips along the mane with sharp pointed scissors.

13 Stick on a thin sausage of black for the tail. Snip to end to look like tail hair.

14 Dampen the tops of the candy-stick legs. Carefully position the body on top of the legs, making sure it is balanced. Gently push the body on to the legs.

Giraffe

Materials:

For this model you will need to use strengthened edible modelling paste (see page 4)

25g (just under 1oz) yellow edible modelling paste

35g (1¼oz) blue edible modelling paste

Five candy sticks

10g (⅓oz) orange sugarpaste

Tiny amount of black sugarpaste

Tools:

Cocktail stick

Sharp pointed scissors

Thin palette knife

Tiny blossom cutter

Instructions:

1 To make the legs, make thin sausages of orange paste and stick them around four candy sticks, making one stripe on each leg.

2 Make the neck from a shortened candy stick with four orange stripes.

3 Shape most of the blue modelling paste into a drum. Keep a tiny piece for later. Stick four pea-sized pieces of orange paste on the top of the drum. Use one of the candy sticks to push a hole down through each ball, ready for inserting the legs. Push each leg through an orange ball and right down into the drum making sure that they are pushed right through to the work surface, and all standing straight.

4 Divide the yellow paste, setting aside a small ball for the head, then shape the rest into a large oval for the body.

5 Shape the head into a pear shape. Mark the nostrils with a cocktail stick. Cut the mouth with sharp pointed scissors.

6 Dampen the top and bottom of the candy-stick neck. Push one end into the body, sticking upwards. Gently push the head on the neck.

7 Make horns from two tiny sausages of orange paste and stick them to the head.

8 Make the ears from two small carrot shapes. Press a line down the middle of each ear, and pinch to a point. Stick to the sides of the head.

9 For the eyes, make a tiny ball of black paste, flatten it and cut it in half. Stick each half on to the head.

10 Decorate the body with orange flowers cut with the tiny blossom cutter. Add blue balls for the flower centres.

11 Make a thin orange sausage for the tail. Mark the end with a knife to make it look like a hairy tail.

12 Dampen the top of the candy-stick legs. Carefully position the body on top of the legs, making sure it is balanced. Gently push the body on to the legs.

Frog

Materials:

25g (just under 1oz) yellow sugarpaste

15g (½oz) green sugarpaste

Small amounts of red and black sugarpaste

Candy stick

Tools:

Cocktail stick

Sharp pointed scissors

Thin palette knife

Plastic sandwich bag

Instructions:

1 For the body, make a narrow oval from 15g (½oz) of yellow paste. Push in a candy stick slightly longer than the body, as support.

2 Make the back from a thin oval of green paste. Roll it slightly longer than the body and stick on to the body, leaving a short point for the stumpy tail.

3 For the legs and arms, make four small balls of yellow and four smaller balls of green. Roll each to form long sausage shapes. Stick the green and yellow together and roll again to make it smooth. Bend each sausage in the middle. Stick two on to the bottom of the body for legs, and two on the top, for arms.

4 For the hands and feet, make four small balls of yellow and four balls of red. Form each to a simple triangle and flatten. Stick the red triangles to the yellow ones. Cut to form four fingers and smooth the cut edges with your fingers. Put the hands and feet into a plastic sandwich bag to stay soft.

5 Make a long oval of green for the head, and a smaller long oval of yellow. Press together and roll each end to a point. Stick the head on top of the body. Mark two little nostrils with a cocktail stick. Position the arms while they are still soft.

6 Stick the hands and feet in position.

7 For the eyes, make two small pea-sized pieces of green. Stick a slightly smaller ball of red on each. Then stick on an even smaller ball of black. Stick the eyes on top of the head.

Acknowledgements
Special thanks to the team at
Search Press for all their hard work:
editor Sophie Kersey, designers
Marrianne Mercer and Juan Hayward
and photographer Debbie Patterson.
Also to Mike for his continuing support
and encouragement.

You are invited to visit the
author's website
www.franklysweet.co.uk